Trust in God but Tie Your Camel

and Other Arab Proverbs

Compiled by Stephen J. McGrane

Foreword by Mohamed I. Ismail, PhD

Llumina
Press

ISBN: 978-1-62550-452-4

Contents

Foreword

The Middle East has been a critical zone throughout history and continues to be so today. Because of the lack of resources and extreme conditions due to geographic location, the people had to adopt unique ways for survival before the Oil Era. Even after black gold (oil), language was the most important means of maintaining their quality of life and providing entertainment. Part of this heritage is the abundant use of proverbs. Arab proverbs reflect the local environment and the life and beliefs of the people. The proverbs collected by Stephen McGrane and published here show how proverbs form the heart of religious, ethical, and social expression in the Arab culture.

Mr. McGrane has done an excellent job of compiling Arab proverbs. Through his experience living in the area while collecting these proverbs, he has shown a global link between the wide-spread use of proverbs in the Middle East and proverbs in the West.

Mr. McGrane is interested in language, as shown especially by his care for proverbs, syntax, and semantics. Though Arabic is not his first language, he has done an excellent job of selecting what is of interest to foreigners as well as to Arab-speaking people. *Trust in God but Tie Your Camel* will interest and entertain both the specialist and the general public.

I hope everyone will benefit from Mr. McGrane's unique work and use it to realize their objectives in many fields. I congratulate him for leading the mission for the benefit of all.

Mohamed I. Ismail, Ph.D.

Kuwait

August 12, 2009

Preface

I was first introduced to Arab proverbs while living in Kuwait in the late 1990s. I heard them in daily conversation and soon started to use them myself. This collection of Arab proverbs is the result of ten years of collecting and recording. These proverbs illuminate the Arab's outlook on life and are published here so that the reader may gain an insight into the Arab culture. This publication is not a scholarly work but rather is intended to entertain while gaining a new perspective.

Proverbs are cultural messages. They provide informal insight into a culture since they are usually linked to a value or belief.

All cultures make use of proverbs but none more abundantly than Arab culture. Their proverbs are remarkable for their use of metaphors and rhymes. A person can demonstrate his or her wisdom and enhance their image by using proverbs in their speech. When learning about a culture, you should seek information from all sources, including proverbs. This collection of Arab proverbs will help you understand the Arab culture. If you want to know how Arabs view a certain topic, simply look up the proverbs on the subject. You will notice that many Arab proverbs have very similar Western equivalents, reflecting our shared values. In fact many of our Western proverbs originated with the Arabs. Many Arab proverbs were adopted by the Hebrew culture and included in the Bible, then disseminated around the world with the spread of Christianity.

The meanings of some of the proverbs are given, if they are not obvious. However, some proverbs can have different meanings in different Arab-speaking countries. If a proverb is only known to be used in one country, the country is noted. Also, the equivalent Western or American proverb, if there is one, is given in quotes.

Stephen J. McGrane

Chapter 1: Family

The son of a duck is a floater.

"Like father, like son."

*If your loved one is made of honey,
don't lick him all up.*

"If you go to a well too many times, the well
will go dry."

ॐ

Raising children is like chewing on a stone.

ॐ

A loved one's onion is a feast.

When your son is young, discipline him;
when he grows older, be a brother to him.
(This saying is attributed to Ja'far Ibn Abi Taleb,
one of the Prophet Mohammed's companions.)

৯৶৽

The son of a son is dear,
the son of a daughter a stranger.

৯৶৽

The son of your son is yours;
the son of your daughter is not.

3

If you come back from a journey, offer your family something, though it be only a stone.

ঙ৹৵৽

Your relatives have first claim on your favors.

"Charity begins at home."

ঙ৹৵৽

The knife of the family does not cut.

Do not be offended if you are harmed by a relative.

*I curse my son and hate
the one who says Amen.*

You can criticize your family, but outsiders
cannot, nor agree with you when you do.

It also means that when you curse your
son it does not mean you hate him.

ॐ

He who reproduces does not die.

ॐ

*He who digs a hole for his brother
will fall into it.*

5

In the eye of his mother,
the monkey is a gazelle.

"All her geese are swans."

There is nothing quite like motherly love.

৩৩৩

Beatings by a loved one
are as sweet as raisins.

৩৩৩

Whoever gets between the onion and its
skin will only be rewarded by its stink.

Never get between a husband and wife,
friends, family members, etc.

*When a man's mother is at home,
his loaf of bread is warm.*

৯৩৫

*The wrath of brothers
is fierce and devilish.*

৯৩৫

The young goose is a good swimmer.

"Like father, like son."

Turn the earthen pot upside down;
the girl will still be like her mother.

"Like mother, like daughter."

Chapter 2: Collectiveness

Birds alight among their like.

"Birds of a feather flock together."

My brother and I against my cousin;
my cousin and I against the stranger.

"Blood is thicker than water."

❧

Help your brother, whether he is an
oppressor or he is oppressed.
(This saying is attributed to the Prophet Mohammed.)

This proverb is often attributed to the Prophet Mohammed. However, it is a pre-Islamic proverb which represents the old Arab way of supporting blood relations and tribes. According to Hadiths (*sayings*) Bukhari and Muslim, when the Prophet Mohammed used this proverb he was asked by his companions how they could support an oppressor and the Prophet responded, "By preventing him from oppressing others," thereby reversing the old adage. However, the original is still used in some quarters today.

Support your brother, whether he is the tyrant or the tyrannized.

This is another version of the previous proverb. It can be traced to Ahmad ibn Hanbal (780-855 A.D.), founder of the Hanbali school of law, who said that leaders were placed in their positions by God and therefore had to be obeyed despite their actions, "even if they are not upright, just, and pious." For ibn Hanbal, it was more important to maintain social order.

૭∘৬

The hand of God is with the group.
(This saying is adopted from the Prophet Mohammed's saying "Blessing and prosperity is with the group.")

There is strength in unity.

11

One hand does not clap.

"It takes two to tango."

Cooperation is essential.

৵৽ড়

*I speak to my daughter-in-law
so my neighbor will hear.*

Because of the collective nature of a culture where
everyone knows everyone else's business, if you don't
want to say something to someone directly, just say it to
someone else and the word will get to them.

Chapter 3: Fate and Luck

Death rides a fast camel.

*It is not every time that
the clay pot survives.*

Don't tempt providence.

❧

*Man does not attain everything he
deserves; winds do not always blow as the
vessels wish.*

❧

A better one in another one.

Better luck next time.

What comes this way goes this way.

"Easy come, easy go."

✎

Tomorrow there will be apricots.

"Tomorrow will be a brighter day."

Used on days when the food is not so good.

✎

The barber opened his shop; his first customer was bald.

Bad luck.

15

What the wind brings
the storm takes away.

"One hand gives and the other takes away."

೭∞ఈ

Spend what is in your pocket;
you will get more from the unknown.

God will provide.

೭∞ఈ

Today's egg is better
than tomorrow's chicken.

"A bird in the hand is worth two in the bush."

Seven trades but no luck.

Even if a person is qualified in many trades, because of
bad luck he may not find work.

෨ඏ

*The Lord sends almonds
to those without teeth.*

Good things come to people
when they are too old to enjoy them.

෨ඏ

Fate is vengeful.

The eye cannot rise above the eyebrow.

જ્જ

The world is changeable, one day honey and the next day onions.

જ્જ

Every sun has to set.

Fame and fortune may be fleeting.

It's all fate and chance.

৯৽৶

Diligence is the mother of good luck.

৯৽৶

Throw a lucky man in the sea and he will come up with fish in his mouth.
(UAE)

Anything that happens once does not necessarily happen again, everything that happens twice is likely to happen for the third time as well.

༄

What is written on the forehead, the eye must see.

Everyone's fate is already written for them to see.

༄

Whatever is written on the forehead is always seen.
(Palestinian version of above.)

Chapter 4: Fear

Fear can make a donkey attack a lion.

Fear those who are afraid of you.

❧

The lion is a coward in strange lands.

❧

*If you conduct yourself
properly, fear no one.*

Chapter 5: God and Religion

If dogs' prayers were answered,
the skies would rain bones.

God can see a black ant walk on a black stone in a black night.

God sees everything.

༶

It came, and God brought it.

Everything comes from God.

༶

No worries, and supplication is to God.

Trust God to remove your worries.

A concealed sin is two-thirds forgiven.

୨୦୶

The slave (man) does the thinking and the Lord (God) carries it out.

"Man proposes and God disposes."

୨୦୶

Bounties are from God.

All good things come from God.

Trust in God, but tie your camel.

"God helps those who help themselves."

According to legend, a man once asked the Prophet Mohammed, who wore armor in battle even though he was protected by God, "Should I tie my camel to the post or should I put my trust in God?" The Prophet responded, "Tie it up and put your trust in God."

&

God is beautiful, and he loves beauty.
(This saying is attributed to the Prophet Mohammed.)

&

Faith moves mountains.

Have faith in a stone,
and you will be healed.

෨෧

Sinning is the best part of repentance.

෨෧

Sins of omission are seldom fun.

27

Fear not the man who fears God.
(Saudi Arabia)

❧

None of you will be considered believers if you do not love your neighbor as yourself.
(This saying is attributed to the prophet Mohammed.)

"You shall love your neighbor as yourself."
The Holy Bible, Leviticus 19:18*

Chapter 6: Wealth and Poverty

Because I have been thirsty, I will dig a well so others may drink.

If you have much, give of your wealth; if you have little, give of your heart.

৵৶

Save your bright penny for a dark day.

"Save for a rainy day."

৵৶

A beggar, and he bargains!

"Beggars can't be choosers."

Unlawful money does not last.

"Ill-gotten gains seldom prosper."

৯৽

*He who has paid his debts
can close his eyes.*

৯৽

Money is a salve.

If a rich man ate a snake, they would say it was because of his wisdom; if a poor man ate it, they would say it was because of his stupidity.

୨୦୶

Money delivers the genie bound.

"He who pays the piper calls the tune."

୨୦୶

If begging should unfortunately be thy lot, knock at the large gates only.

He that loves silver is never satisfied with silver; he that loves luxury will gain no profit form it. This is also vanity!
(This saying is attributed to the Prophet Mohammad.)

"He who loves silver will not be satisfied with silver; nor he who loves abundance, with increase. This also is vanity."
The Holy Bible, Ecclesiastes 5:10

৩৯৹

The rich man has many friends.

"The poor man is hated even by his own neighbor, but the rich has many friends."
The Holy Bible, Proverbs 14:20

One coin in the moneybox makes more noise than when it is full.

❧

One can reach nobility even if his clothes are tattered and his pocket is patched.

❧

The soul desires more if you encourage it, but it returns to contentment when it is disciplined.

Be happy with what you have.

Chapter 7: Business

*Only a fool tests the depth
of water with both feet.*

Minimize your risk.

It is both a social and a business call.

This proverb reflects the Arab tendency
to mix business with pleasure.

❧

Unattended money teaches theft.

❧

*There is not a tree that has not been
swayed by the breeze.*

Everyone has a price.

If you buy cheap meat, you will be sorry when you come to the gravy.

৩০৬

Live together like brothers and do business like strangers.

৩০৬

Make your bargain before beginning to plow.

Do not buy a fish in the water.

"Don't buy a pig in a poke."

❧

It's like selling fish still in the sea.

"Don't count your chickens
before they are hatched."

❧

*Give the bread to the baker,
even if he eats half of it.*

It is better to hire a specialist.

*Sell what you have while the
dust is still on your shoes.*
(Palestine)

৯৶৶

*A little debt makes a debtor,
a great one an enemy.*

৯৶৶

*The fruit of timidity
is neither gain nor loss.*

Chapter 8: Work

Exert effort. You shall be rewarded.

Tire out your body, but not your mind.

❧

Wishing does not make a poor man rich.

❧

Dwell not upon thy weariness; thy strength shall be according to the measure of thy desire.

Tire yourself out for the sake of something and you shall get it.

*He who relies on his
brother's loaf dies of hunger.*

ॐ∽ॐ

Don't leave today's work until tomorrow.

"Never put off 'til tomorrow
what can be done today."

ॐ∽ॐ

*He who perseveres finds,
and he who sows harvests.*

*If you cannot have a government job,
wallow in its dust.*
(I have only heard this used in Egypt.)

Government jobs are the best.

৵৽

*Pay the employee his remuneration before
his sweat dries out.*
(This saying is attributed to the Prophet Mohammed.)

Chapter 9: Heritage

When you come to the desert, you cry;
when you leave, you cry even more.

Lost is the person who forgets his or her past. (Egypt)

৵৽

Faith is Yemeni; wisdom is Yemeni.
(This saying is attributed to the Prophet Mohammed.)

Read history as it is filled with morals. A nation will sink if it knows nothing of its annals.

Also, *"Recount to them these parables, so that they may take thought."*
The Holy Koran, The Heights 7:176*

"Those who cannot remember the past are condemned to repeat it."
George Santayana, Spanish Poet

*Passages from *The Holy Koran* are from translation by N. J. Dawood.

Chapter 10: Rhetoric

When eyes meet, the tongue becomes shy.

It's easier to talk behind someone's
back than to his or her face.

What comes from the lips
reaches the lips; what comes
from the heart reaches the heart.

❧

A man's tongue is his sword.

❧

Your tongue is your horse; if you use it
right, it'll save you and if you betray it, it
will betray you.

Arabs are taught to use words wisely and forcefully.

Your tongue is like a horse—if you take care of it, it takes care of you; if you treat it badly, it treats you badly.
(another version of the above)

❧❧

If I have regretted my silence once, I have regretted my chatter many times.

❧❧

A man profits more by the sight of an idiot than by the orations of the learned.

❧❧

Talk has a taste like food.

Sit crooked and speak straight.

❧

The ass that goes to Mecca remains an ass.

A place or forum does not make
you or your words better.

❧

*An intelligent deaf-mute is better than an
ignorant person who can speak.*

"Better to be silent and thought a fool than open
your mouth and remove all doubt."

*Examine what is said,
not him who speaks.*

❧

*It is good to know the truth, but it is
better to speak of palm trees.*

Do not reveal all that you know.

❧

*When you shoot an arrow of truth, dip its
point in honey.*

Insults should be written in sand; compliments should be carved in stone.

৩৯৩

If speech is silver, silence is golden.

"Silence is golden; speech is silver."

৩৯৩

The fruit of silence is tranquility.

৩৯৩

No answer is an answer.

Silence is the best answer to the stupid. The fool has his answer on the tip of his tongue.

ೞഔ

Lower your voice and strengthen your argument.
(Lebanon)

ೞഔ

The wound of words is worse than the wound of swords.

"The pen is mightier than the sword."

Chapter 11: Age and Experience

Instruction in youth is like engraving in stone.
(Morocco)

Ask the experienced, not the learned.

❧

Older than you by a day,
wiser than you by a year.

Respect older people and their advice.

❧

To every horse a stumble,
and to every sage a lapse.

"Nobody is perfect."

Experiences are the glasses of the mind.

৵৹

*Ask one who has experience
rather than a physician.*

"Experience without learning is better than
learning without experience."

৵৹

He who grows with a habit grays with it.

"Old habits die hard."

The tongue of experience is more truthful.

&

Shall the gosling teach the goose to swim?

&

What is learnt in the
cradle lasts to the grave.

&

No man is a good physician
who has never been sick.

Chapter 12: Patience

Slower than a turtle.
(UAE)

Patience is beautiful.

❧

Grapes are eaten one by one.

❧

Patience is bitter, but its fruit is sweet.

Diligence is a great teacher.
(UAE)

❧❧

A journey of a thousand miles starts with one step.

❧❧

Haste is the devil's work, and patience is from God.

"Patience is a virtue."

*No matter how fast the poplar grows, it
will never reach heaven.*
(Lebanon)

❧

*Time is like a sword, if you
do not cut it, it will cut you.*

Wasting time can have disastrous consequences.

❧

The hasty and the tardy meet at the ferry.
(UAE)

"Too swift arrives as tardy as too slow."
William Shakespeare

The hasty angler loses the fish.

৽৽৽

The hasty hand catches frogs for fish.

৽৽৽

Patience is the key to relief.

Thankfulness, remembrance, and patience.
In them are blessings and rewards.

ജ

The difficult is done at once;
the impossible takes a little longer.

Chapter 13: Power

The strong man is not he who overcomes others, but he who overcomes his own anger.
(This saying is attributed to the Prophet Mohammed.)

"Who is mighty?
He who overcomes his impulse."
Ethics of the Fathers, 4:1

*Show your enemy your
sword and your gold.*

Expresses the carrot-and-stick approach to tribal power.

ॐ

*If you are a peg, endure the knocking; if
you are a mallet, strike.*
(Morocco)

ॐ

Anger is an ember from the fire.
(This saying is attributed to the Prophet Mohammad)

"The angry man is replete with poison."
Confucius

Chapter 14: Health

After dinner, rest;
after supper, walk a mile.

Stephen J. McGrane

He who has health has hope, and he who has hope has everything.

❧

Hygiene is two-thirds of health.
(Lebanon)

70

Chapter 15: Friendship

Stay with your old crony,
even if the new friend enriches you.

Old friends are best.

The enemy of my enemy is my friend.

୨∞୧

*If a pot is cooking,
the friendship will stay warm.*

୨∞୧

A true friend is for the time of trouble.

A friend is known when needed.

෨෧

*Give your friend your
blood and your money.*

෨෧

*The world is a rose;
smell it and pass it on to your friends.*
(Palestine)

Chapter 16: Marriage, Love, and Beauty

A fat woman is a blanket for winter.

A woman can hide her love for forty years,
but her disgust and anger not for one day.

❧

Even a one-eyed guy
will wink at a beautiful woman.

❧

The weapon of a woman is her tears.

Don't trust a woman when she cries.

Her face sours the milk.

৯৩

*Love sees sharply, hatred sees even more
sharp, but jealousy sees the sharpest, for it
is love and hate at the same time.*

৯৩

*He married the monkey for its money;
the money went, and
the monkey stayed a monkey.*

The whisper of a pretty girl can be heard further than the roar of a lion.

৩৩৬

Marriage is like a fort, those who are in want out, those who are out want in.

৩৩৬

What can the lady comber do with this ugly face?

"You cannot make a silk purse out of a sow's ear."

Work for the engagement of your daughter, but don't work for the engagement of your son.

✿

Evening promises are like butter; morning comes and it's all melted.
(Morocco)

✿

A beautiful thing is never perfect.
(Egypt)

A bald woman brags about her niece's hair.

৭০৵ও

Please make no mistake, we are not shy;
we really know our worth, the moon and I.

Used to tell a girl she is prettier than the moon.

৭০৵ও

She says to the moon, "Disappear; and I
shall take your place."

She is as beautiful as the moon.

Chapter 17: Honesty

You stole the chicken;
the feather is on your head.

Being caught red-handed.

*Beware the man who
you have only seen smile.*
(Egypt)

❧

Beware: some liars tell the truth.

❧

*Lie to a liar, for lies are his coin; steal from
a thief, for that is easy; lay a trap for a
trickster and catch him at first attempt,
but beware of an honest man.*

The rope of a lie is short.

৵৵৽

He steals the kohl (makeup) from the eye.

"He'd steal the shirt off your back."

৵৵৽

If the lion bares his teeth,
don't assume he is smiling.

Things are not always what they appear.

He who steals the egg steals the camel.

If someone would steal something small,
he will steal bigger things also.

৽৽৻

*If you want to be a liar,
better have a good memory.*

৽৽৻

*A man is not honest simply because he
never had a chance to steal.*
(Yemen)

Chapter 18: Miscellaneous

An army of sheep led by a lion would defeat an army of lions led by a sheep.

On the day of victory no one is tired.

❧

A known mistake is better than an unknown truth.

❧

The boat that brings you back is far superior to that which takes you away.
(Egypt)

Reflects Egyptians desire to return to Egypt.

He who drinks the water of the Nile is destined to taste its sweetness again. (Egypt)

Egypt is so wonderful that visitors will want to return.

৩৹◌⋖

The dogs may bark but the caravan moves on.

A person should rise above petty criticism.

৩৹◌⋖

*Let trouble (evil) alone,
and trouble will let you alone.*

"Don't trouble trouble till trouble troubles you."

When the wolf comes for the sheep, the dog goes to defecate.

When you need someone the most they are not around.

❧

The last resort is the hot rod.

"Desperate diseases must
have desperate remedies."

❧

Farther than earth from heaven.

Used to point out that two things
being compared are very different.

A book is a garden in your pocket.

❧

Reading books removes
sorrows from the heart.
(Morocco)

❧

False ambition serves the neck.
(Egypt)

When the angels present themselves, the devils abscond.
(Egypt)

❧

The stone which the builders rejected has become the headstone of the corner.

"The stone which the builders rejected has become the chief cornerstone."
The Holy Bible, Psalms 118:22

❧

The waters wear away the stones.

"As water wears away stones, …"
The Holy Bible, Job 14:19

He who sows doubt may eat or he may not.

৽৽৽

She went looking for horns and returned home without ears.

While looking for something you lost,
you loose something else.

৽৽৽

The borrowed robe doesn't keep out the cold.

You feel better using your own things.

A little and a little, collected together, makes a great deal; the heap in the barn consists of single grains, and drops of rain make an inundation.
(Saudi Arabia)

৯৽৻

When they came to shove the horse of the sultan, the beetle came along and stuck out her foot.

When you expect an important person
to do something you might find it has already
been done by a lowly person.

What taught the donkeys to ear ginger?

Offering something of value to
someone who doesn't appreciate it.

❧

To cast pearls before swine.

Same as above.

❧

A man with one plan goes out to execute it; a man with two plans becomes perplexed.

If your messenger tarries, expect good.

ༀ

A promise is a cloud; fulfillment is rain.

ༀ

All sunshine makes the desert.

"All sunshine and no rain make the desert."

There has to be bad with the good.
(Another proverb the West has gotten from Arabs.)

*Dawn does not come
twice to awaken a man.*

஽

Example is better than precept.

"Leadership by example."

஽

Never give advice in a crowd.

Never sit in the place of a man who can say to you, "Rise."

❧

Never speak ill of the dead.

❧

On the first of March, the crows begin to search.

Sad are only those who understand.

৯৯৯

Every head has its own headache.

৯৯৯

Write bad things that are done to you in sand, but write the good things that happen to you on a piece of marble.

Follow the advice of those who make you cry, never of those who make you laugh.

൧∞ൟ

Make sure you have a different opinion and people will talk about you.

൧∞ൟ

Silence is medication for sorrow.

The dream of a cat is filled with mice.

๑๏๑

Habit is the 6th sense
that overrules the other 5.

๑๏๑

It is wise to bring some water when one
goes out to look for water.

We learn little from our successes, but a lot from our failures.

❧

He made a dome from a seed.

"He made a mountain out of a mole hill."

❧

He who watches others obsessively dies of chagrin.

The camel limped from its split lip.

"A bad workman blames his tools."

❧

Choose the neighbor before the house.

We can live without friends but not without neighbors.

❧

*He who chooses too
large a stone cannot strike with it.*

"Don't bite off more than you can chew."

Still a goat, even if she flies.

৵৽৹

A man is known by his manners, not by his clothes.

"Clothes don't make the man."

৵৽৹

What is past is dead.

"Let bygones be bygones."

Live with us then judge us.

❧

*The clouds are not hurt
by the baying of dogs.*

"Dogs barking at the moon."

❧

From under the drip to under the spout.

"Out of the pan and into the fire."

O departing one, leave behind good deeds.

"A good deed is never lost."

❧

*He is like a deaf person
at a wedding procession.*

"A fish out of water."

❧

*The day obliterates the
promises of the night.*

"Vows made in storms are forgotten in calms."

He who does not recognize
the falcon grills it.

❧

No smoke without fire.

"Where there's smoke there's fire."

❧

He who lives beside the blacksmith is
branded by his fire.

105

*I become the slave of he
who teaches me one letter.*

❧

*The hungry man dreams
of the bread market.*

❧

We mention the cat, it came bounding.

"Speak of the devil."

Be contrary and be known.

๛

The goat's stall in your own house is better than your neighbor's palace.

"There's no place like home."

๛

The camel cannot see its own hump.

"The pot calls the kettle black."

The best deeds are those done promptly.

❧

When stomachs are busy minds are lost.

❧

The mind is for seeing,
the heart is for hearing.

Too many captains sink the ship.

"Too many cooks spoil the broth."

৩৵৶

The camel's dung points to the camel.

৩৵৶

We taught them how to beg,
they raced us to the gates.

To beat someone at his own game.

The dog's tail remains crooked, even if it is put in fifty moulds.

"A leopard cannot change its spots."

჻

Cleanliness is akin to faith.
(This saying is attributed to the Prophet Mohammed.)

"Cleanliness is next to Godliness."

჻

It's like a public bath with its water cut off.

Chaos.

Every sun has its sunset.

"All good things must come to an end."

༄

He whose eye is greedy
will never have a full stomach.

Some people are never satisfied.

༄

He who has his hand in the water is not
like him who has his hand in the fire.

111

A wise man will not be bitten from a hole twice.
(This saying comes from a saying attributed to the Prophet Mohammed: "A believer will not be bitten from a hole twice.")

"Once bitten, twice shy."

❧

He pretends to be humble until he has his chance.

❧

I am a prince and you are a prince, so who will drive the donkeys?

"All chiefs and no Indians."

*Eat what pleases you
and wear what pleases others.*

"Say as men say, but think for yourself."

৯৶ড়

A tent cannot be put up with one peg.

৯৶ড়

Go tile the sea.

"Go jump in the lake."

Get lost.

The fish ate the bait and stole the hook.

"To add insult to injury."

❧❦

The envious will not prevail.

❧❦

I have neither a male nor a female camel in it.

"It's no skin off my nose."
"I don't have a dog in the fight."

From a lack of horses they saddled dogs.

A useless alternative.

❧⚜❧

*He who wants to drown
his dog accuses him of mange.*

❧⚜❧

The eloquent cock crows from the egg.

He hit me and cried;
he raced me to complain.

෨෦෯

Stretch your legs according
to the length of your quilt.

"Cut your coat according to your cloth."

෨෦෯

The key to evil is one word.

*If it was going to rain
it would have clouded over.*

৩৵৵৵

Tie the donkey where his master tells you.

৩৵৵৵

He who sows the wind harvests the storm.

"Whatever a man sows, that he will also reap."
The Holy Bible, Galatians 6:7

A donkey is a donkey
even if he is raised among horses.

❧

Beware the evil of the man who has
received your charity.

❧

Two watermelons cannot
be carried in one hand.

Don't attempt the impossible.

Every day has its blessings.
(This saying is attributed to the Prophet Mohammed.)

"Every cloud has a silver lining."

❧

He comes to apply makeup to the eye and blinds it.

"To kill with kindness."

❧

Rather a bird in the hand than ten on the tree.

"A bird in the hand is worth two in the bush."

119

We say "It's a bull,' he says, "Milk it."

"Don't confuse me with the facts."

❧

He gives earrings to the one without ears.

❧

*If you don't understand it with a wink,
you certainly will with a blow.*
(Morocco)

Like a bride's mother.

"Busy as a bee."

৯৶৻

*He who chews with his
own teeth benefits himself.*

"God helps those who help themselves."

৯৶৻

*Every cock is a town crier
on his own dung heap.*

Both a pilgrim and a seller of prayer beads.

"Jack of all trades."

৵৽ঌ

If a gazelle falls ill do not send the lion to diagnose the complaint.

Use the right person for the job.

৵৽ঌ

He who does not attend his goats during delivery will not be given twins.

Mind your shop.

Every house has its sewers.

ৡৎ

They criticized the rose,
they said its cheek was red.

Some people can find fault in anything.

ৡৎ

Everyone puts his own
loaf as close as he can to the fire.

Look out for number one.

The prayer beads have come unstrung.

"The fat is in the fire."

❧

Sixty years, seventy days.

"Six in one, half a dozen in the other."

❧

He asked "What could be cheaper than honey?" – vinegar is free.

Every garment has a fault.

Nothing is perfect.

୨୦୶

*We let him in and he
brought his donkey too.*

"Give him an inch and he'll take a mile."

୨୦୶

Every knot has someone to undo it.

*There is nothing after
hardship except repose.*

This saying is taken from a verse in *The Holy Koran*:
"Every hardship is followed by ease."
(*The Holy Koran*, Comfort 94:4)

❧

*If the hammer does not
break it, the saw will cut it.*

❧

At the knot the carpenter stopped.

"Throwing in the towel."

Nothing is for free, not even blindness and deafness.

৯৽৽

When the branch is out of reach he says, "Your grapes are sour!"

"Sour grapes."

Disparaging what one cannot obtain.
Originates from the Greek writer Aesop's famous fable
"*The Fox and the Grapes.*"

Do not bind a generous man with conditions.

"Don't look a gift horse in the mouth."

You can estimate the age or value of a horse by looking in its mouth (at its teeth) but, as with any gift, you should be grateful no matter what the value.

৲৵৶

A thousand curses do not tear a robe.

"Sticks and stones may break my bones but words will never hurt me."

৲৵৶

The kid teaches its mother to suckle.

If you stop every time a dog barks, your road will never end.

Stephen J. McGrane

Keep away from trouble and sing to it.

❧

As you went, so you came back.

❧

They left the cat to guard the milk.

"The fox is guarding the henhouse."

The daughter of the house is one-eyed.

"The grass is greener on the other side."

ৎৡৡ৵

Let the watermelons break each other.

"Let them stew in their own juices."

ৎৡৡ৵

The room is small and the donkey is a kicker.

"This place is not big enough for both of us."

He pulled the carpet from under his feet.

❧

A fire in the heart but no tear in the eye.

"To keep a stiff upper lip."

❧

*The people of Mecca know
their own streets best.*

Your guilt stands at your side.

❧

The ignorant person is his own enemy.

❧

If the cow falls, the knives multiply.

"To kick someone when they are down."

The idle man makes himself a judge.

৶৽৻

Like a snake under the hay.

"Like a snake in the grass."

৶৽৻

It is the business of the muezzin to call to prayers.

"Mind your own business."

Walls have ears.

৽৽৽

The wound that bleeds inwardly is the most dangerous.

৽৽৽

After the incense is passed there is no sitting on.

Don't overstay your welcome.

135

The one-eyed person is a beauty in the country of the blind.

"In the land of the blind,
the one-eyed man is king."

❧

Into the well from which you drink, do not throw a stone.

❧

A single grain tips the scales.

"The last straw breaks the camel's back."

*Your right hand doesn't know
what your left hand is doing.*
(This saying is attributed to the Prophet Mohammed.)

৩৯৬৯

*When the lions were absent,
the hyenas played.*

"When the cat's away, the mice will play."

৩৯৬৯

*The butcher is not alarmed by the
multitude of sheep.*

"The more the merrier."

137

The water shows up the diver.

"The proof is in the pudding."

❧

Enter houses by their front doors.

Don't do things behind someone's back.

❧

Longer than the fasting month.

The words "I wish" built no houses.

"If wishes were horses beggars would ride."

❧

He struck two birds with one stone.

❧

He who seeks higher things stays awake at night.

A new sieve is taunt.

"A new broom sweeps clean."

୨∘ଈ

A dog that barks does not bite.

"His bark is worse than his bite."

୨∘ଈ

What you cannot see during the day, you cannot see at night.
(Sudan)

*The man who is in the right has both
stature and the last word.*

ക്ക

*A man should live if only
to satisfy his curiosity.*
(Yemen)

ക്ക

Learn politeness from the impolite.
(Egypt)

The dream of cats is all mice.

༐

The hunter seethes and the bird preens.

One is unaffected by the desperation of others.

༐

Both the line and the bird have gone.

He ate the camel and all it carried.

"To eat someone out of house and home."

❧

A drowning man clutches at a straw.

❧

His greed killed him.

Add wetness to the mud.

"Add fuel to the fire."

❧

Frankness is peace of mind.

❧

*Every decayed bean has
a one-eyed man to weigh it.*

A clever woman could spin with a donkey's foot.

❧

The eye sees but the hand does not reach.

❧

Trust makes way for treachery.

*The barking dog does not
disturb the man on a camel.*
(Egypt)

କ୍ଟ

*Do today what you
want to postpone tomorrow.*
(Lebanon)

"Don't put off to tomorrow
what you can do today."

କ୍ଟ

His brains hang at the top of his fez.
(Lebanon)

Do not cut down the tree
that gives you shade.
(UAE)

೪ೲ

Death is a black camel that lies down at
every door. Sooner or later you must ride
the camel.
(UAE)

೪ೲ

Death is a black camel which
kneels at every man's gate.

147

Compete, don't envy.

৩৯৩

Visit rarely and you will be more loved.
(This saying is attributed to the Prophet Mohammed.)

"Don't wear out your welcome."

৩৯৩

A kind word can attract
even the snake from his nest.
(UAE)

The book that remains shut is but a block.
(UAE)

৵৽

*A little body doth often
harbor a great soul.*

Time runs

"Time flies."

❧

A fool sees not the same tree that a wise man sees.
(UAE)

❧

A drowning man is not troubled by rain.
(UAE)

All mankind is divided into three classes: those that are immovable, those that are moveable, and those that move.

༺⚬༻

A broken hand works but not a broken heart.
(UAE)

༺⚬༻

Be generous to a generous person and you'd win him; be generous to a mean person and he'd rebel on you.
(UAE)

151

Do good to people and you'll
enslave their hearts.
(UAE)

৯৽৽৩

Be aware of the idiot, for he is like an old
dress. Every time you patch it, the wind
will tear it back again.
(UAE)

৯৽৽৩

Judge a man by the
reputation of his enemies.
(UAE)

Judge not a ship as she lies on the stocks.

"Don't judge a book by its cover."

༺∞༺

*You are like a tree, giving
your shade to the outside.*

༺∞༺

*The best answer comes from
the man who isn't angry.*
(UAE)

153

Throw dirt enough and some will stick.

❧

Beware of one who flatters unduly;
he will also censure unjustly.

❧

Never justify yourself, your enemies won't
believe you and your friends won't need it.

❧

It is in time of testing that a man becomes
an object of derision or respect.

When its time has arrived, the prey becomes the hunter.
(Palestine)

❧

To follow a multitude.

"You shall not follow a crowd to do evil."
The Holy Bible, Exodus 23:2

❧

If only I were a bird!
Ah, but eating caterpillars?
(Palestine)

The bad with the good.

155

Away from the eye, away from the mind.
(Palestine)

"Out of sight, out of mind."

❧

*Knowledge is a treasure
but practice is the key to it.*

❧

*There is no point in running:
one should leave on time.*

Salt will never be worm-eaten.

❧❧

The different sorts of
madness are innumerable.

❧❧

Search for knowledge
though it be in China.

Think of going out before you enter.

❧

When a door opens not to your knock,
consider your reputation.

❧

When what you want does not happen,
learn to want what does.

What does not go with you, goes with him.

৩৽৻

Metaphor is the bridge to reality.

This proverb is illustrated in *The Holy Koran* where human attributes are often used to understand God.

159

Also by Stephen J. McGrane: *Sit Crooked and Speak Straight: Doing Business on the Arabian Peninsula.* Llumina Press, ISBN: 978-1-60594-031-1, Paperback, 168 pages, 2008. http://sitcrookedandspeakstraight.com/

www.ingramcontent.com/pod-product-compliance
Lightning Source LLC
Chambersburg PA
CBHW030015290326
41934CB00005B/354